CATS

Darren Bennett

HarperCollins*Publishers*

First published in 1993
by HarperCollins*Publishers*, London
Reprinted 1994, 1995, 1996, 1998

© Diagram Visual Information 1993

Editor: Margaret Doyle
Art Director: Darren Bennett
Contributing artists: Laura Andrew, James Dallas,
Ryozo Kohira, Kyri Kyriacou, Lee Lawrence, Ali Marshall,
Philip Patenall, Jane Robertson, Amanda Williams

A catalogue record for this book is available from the British Library

ISBN 0 00 412669 6

Printed and bound by New Man Wah Printing Co., Ltd., Hong Kong

CONTENTS

Tools and Equipment

Pencils

You'll find that pencils are the most versatile tools for drawing. There are many types, and each creates different effects. They can be used for both preliminary sketches and final artwork.

Pencils are categorized by hardness – from 9B, the softest, up to 9H, the hardest. The harder the pencil, the sharper the line it makes; soft pencils, in contrast, make heavier, thicker lines. This variation is especially useful when drawing different kinds of fur on cats.

Among the many types of pencil are clutch and propelling pencils and coloured pencils.

You can erase easily with pencil, and by rubbing over your marks with your finger you can create smudges and blended areas for a soft effect. Final pencil drawings must be sprayed with a fixative to prevent accidental smudging.

Learn about the range of effects you can produce by trying the different types of pencil available.

The soft, sketchy outlines of this cat (*below left*) were made with B pencil on cartridge paper

Notice the level of detail that can be obtained using a pen, as in this drawing of a striped tabby done on plastic film using a fineline ball-point pen

Pens

Pens also come in a range of types that produce distinctive effects.

Ball-point pens are good for both sketching and final artwork but can produce blotchy lines if you are not careful.

Felt-tip pens and **studio markers** come in many different thicknesses. They are good for bold, strong drawings, especially when vibrant colour is wanted.

Fountain and **dip pens** with ink make clear, fluid lines and are good for capturing movement. You can get nibs of different widths and can vary the thickness of the line by applying more or less pressure.

Technical pens are useful for detailed drawings when you want smooth, even lines.

Ink for these pens is available in a range of colours, although black is used most frequently for drawing.

Because pen marks cannot be erased, you might want to start with a sketch in pencil.

Remember to replace the caps on felt-tip pens and studio markers and to clean technical and dip pens after use. Try out different types to see what each can do.

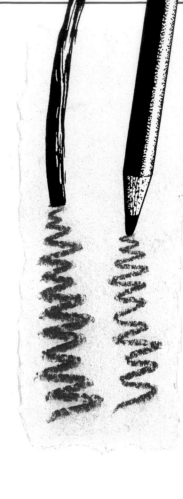

The face of this Siamese cat was drawn on textured Ingres paper using conté crayon

Pastels, crayons and charcoal

Pastels, crayons and charcoal are tools that lend themselves well to drawing cats. You can make a variety of marks with them and, especially when used on rough paper, they give your drawing a lively texture.

Oil-based pastels and **wax-based crayons** are available in a spectrum of vibrant colours. These soft tools are not as good for making detailed drawings, but they can be combined with other media for interesting effects.

Charcoal and **conté crayon** are harder, sometimes brittle tools; they can break easily, so it may take some time to get used to them. You can use the tip to draw fine, detailed lines, and use the side to fill in larger areas.

By rubbing your finger or a piece of kneaded dough in places, you can blend and soften your lines or create white highlights.

I used charcoal on
textured Ingres paper
for this reclining
Siamese

These tools smudge easily, so be careful not to
rest your hand directly on your paper while you
work, and be sure to spray your final drawing
with a fixative.

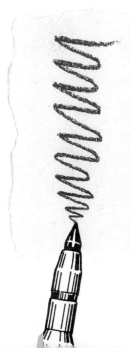

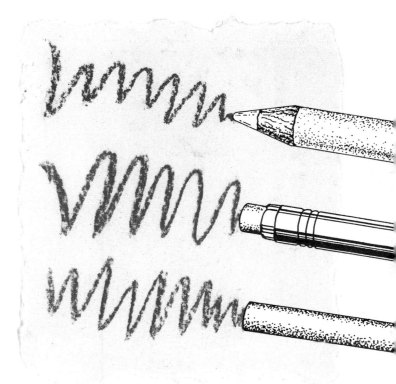

7

Brushes and wet media

Paints and inks are a wonderful way to add colour and soft effects to your drawing.

Brushes come in different thicknesses: those with thin, pointed tips are good for finer detail and lines, and those with flat, wide tips are better for filling in large areas. They are made of sable or squirrel hair (the most expensive types) or of a synthetic fibre.

2

3

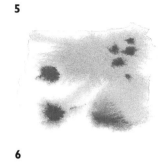

5

4

6

1 These brush strokes show the different effects achieved using watercolour and (*from left to right*) a small, pointed tip; a flat brush; and a large, pointed tip

2 These thick and thin brush strokes show how the tone of watercolour varies by the amount of water used. The more water added, the lighter the tone

Transparent watercolour can be bright or muted; you can create lighter, more transparent colours by adding more water. Lines made by pencil or pen can show through watercolour.
Gouache is opaque watercolour. It creates areas of strong, solid colour and covers any lines on the paper beneath, although the texture of the paper will still come through.
Acrylics are also opaque and are good for strong, vibrant colour. They have a thick consistency but can be thinned with water.
Oils are not water based, so they can be difficult to use. They also take a long time to dry, something to consider if space or time is at a premium.

When using paints and inks, you will need a palette for mixing, jars for water, and a surface on which to place paints and jars. Use relatively thick paper to prevent your drawing from curling or buckling.

3 When painting an area, keep the same tone all over. Start with a light wash, and build up tone while the underlying layer is still wet

4 Painting over dry areas keeps the different layers from blending and creates variations in tone

5 Dampening areas of your paper with a small amount of clean water allows you to create soft edges as the paint spreads and diffuses

6 Adding darker blotches of paint or ink on damp paper creates unusual effects

The portrait of a tortoiseshell cat (*opposite*) was done first in pencil on watercolour paper. The pencil sketch was then covered with a watercolour wash

The tortoiseshell cat in another pose (*right*) was done in watercolour on watercolour paper

Surfaces to draw on

The paper you draw on, like the tool you use, determines the character of your drawing. Paper can be rough or smooth, thick or thin, coloured or white. Certain surfaces combine better with some tools than others. Paints and inks work best on thick, absorbent paper. Charcoal and conté crayon can be used on pastel-coloured paper. For more on the effects of tools and surfaces, see the following pages.

Paper is made in one of three ways.
Handmade paper, although expensive, is of the best quality and is long lasting. It has variations so that each sheet is somewhat different.
Mould paper is formed sheet-by-sheet, like handmade paper, but by a machine. It has a wrong and a right side.
Machine-made paper is of a uniform quality – that is, each sheet is the same. It is produced in a continuous roll and cut into sheets later.

The crisp, clean lines in the Abyssinian's fur were produced using fineline felt-tip pen on smooth tracing paper

Notice the interesting, fuzzy effect created by a rough, textured paper like Bockingford when used with a relatively soft, 2B pencil

The texture of the paper is determined by special treatments. A paper or board that is hot-pressed is smooth; one that is not has a slightly rough texture. Wove and laid papers have a subtle, continuous texture that reflects the pattern of the mould used to form the sheet.

Experiment with many combinations to find which ones best suit you and the style of your drawing.

The markings opposite were made by (*from left to right*) 3B pencil, 2B pencil, felt-tip pen, conté crayon and charcoal.

Newsprint is
inexpensive, making
it good for sketching
and practising

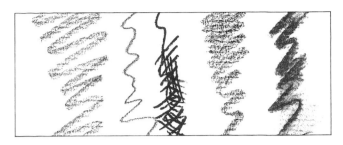

Ingres paper is often used
with charcoal or pastels.
It is available in white and
pale shades

Tracing paper is
semi-transparent so
it lets you trace other
images quickly

Watercolour paper
is thick and absorbent,
so it works well with
wet media

Stationery paper is
usually available in
one standard size. It
works well with pen

Bristol board is
stiff, with a smooth
surface, and is best
for pen drawings

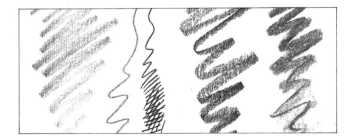

Cartridge paper, usually
textured and of a high
quality, is one of the most
versatile surfaces

Layout paper is a semi-
opaque, lightweight paper
that works best with
pencils and pens

Choosing the Right Medium

The tool you use, the marks you make, and the surface you draw on all combine in unique and interesting ways. The drawings of a tabby cat's face on these pages are identical in their subject, but not in any other way. Each is created by a different combination of tool and surface. You can almost feel the softness of the fur in some. In others, the emphasis is on the shape of the cat's head. Others highlight the details in the markings of the fur.

Practise using different tools on various surfaces. You'll soon learn to predict the effects you can create, allowing you to choose which to use according to the final appearance you are trying to achieve.

1 Soft pencil on cartridge paper
2 Dip pen on cartridge paper
3 Charcoal on rough, coloured paper
4 Ball-point pen on Bristol board
5 Watercolour on watercolour paper
6 Coloured pencil on cartridge paper
7 Hard pencil on cartridge paper
8 Pastel on Ingres paper
9 Felt-tip pen on layout paper

2

3

1

4

5

6

7

8

9

Measuring in Drawing

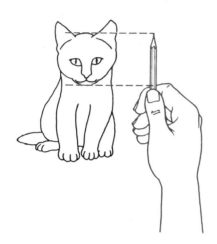

Pencil measuring
Check the accuracy of your drawing by measuring with your pencil. Hold the pencil upright in your outstretched hand. With the point at the top of the object to be measured, move your thumb to the bottom of the object. Keeping your thumb in place, move the pencil to your paper to transfer the measurement.

A useful method when drawing cats is to measure the height of the cat's head and use this as a gauge. See how many of these head heights make up the cat's body. In my drawing below, the kitten's body is one and a half heads high.

One of the easiest mistakes to make, especially when drawing animals, is to misrepresent the relationship among different elements, such as legs, head and body. It helps to understand proportion, which is explained in more detail on pp. 16–17. Here are a few tips for quick ways to check that what you see is what's really there.

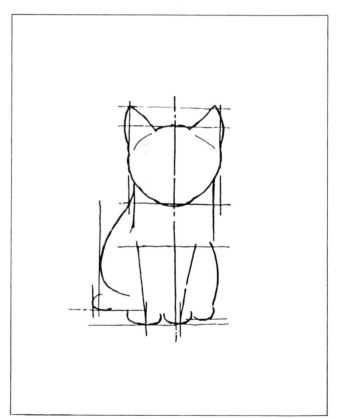

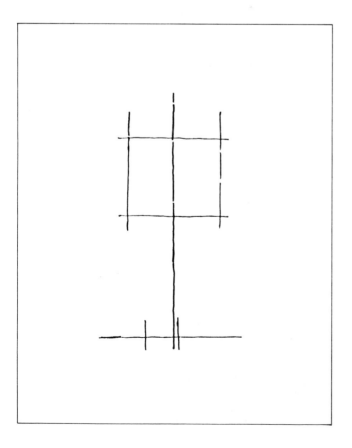

You might be surprised at what you find when using pencil measuring with a central vertical line (*left*) to check your accuracy

I used my pencil to measure the distance from the baseline to the bottom of the chin and the top of the head and ears, drawing horizontal lines at each section (*above*). These horizontals helped me find the right positioning of the kitten's legs in relation to its head

Verticals and horizontals

Another way to check your accuracy is to draw a vertical line down the centre of your page. Use this as the main axis of the cat's body, and relate the positioning of other elements to this vertical. By holding your pencil up vertically, you can see where the cat's shoulders and feet should be placed in relation to this line. The three stages shown on the left illustrate how to build up a drawing from simple verticals and horizontals.

I then used horizontal pencil measuring to help me draw the cat's body in its correct position. I discovered that this kitten's feet are off centre

The final drawing of the kitten (*right*) was drawn using HB and B pencils on cartridge paper

Proportion and Shapes

When drawing cats it helps to understand a few principles of their anatomy.

- A cat's basic body parts are two hind legs, two forelegs, a torso, a neck, and a head. Don't forget the tail, a distinctive feature of most cats.
- A cat's legs are about one-third shorter than the length of its body.
- A cat is usually taller at its hips than at its shoulders.
- A cat's body height is in proportion to its head height.

Getting the proportions right at the basic outline stage is essential.

Seated cat

To draw a seated cat from the front, think of the head in terms of a square and the body as a rectangle in proportion to the head height. The ears are also in proportion to the head.

Use a central vertical line as the main axis, and draw the body in relation to this axis, as described on pp. 14–15. Look carefully at what you can see from this angle. In the drawing below, for example, three paws are visible.

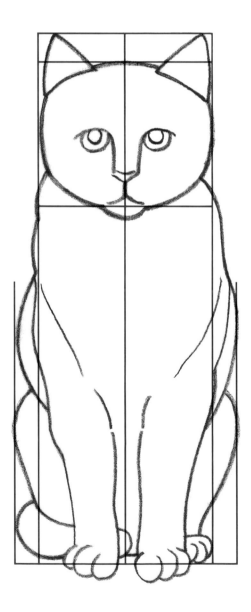

The proportions of a kitten and an adult cat are somewhat different, but the same principles apply to both. When seen from the front in a sitting pose, a full-grown cat's body will be about two and a half times its head height (*left*). A kitten's body in this pose will be less — about one and a half times its head height

The final drawing (*right*) was done in soft pencil on cartridge paper

Standing cat in profile

To draw a standing cat from the side, think of
the head again in terms of a square. The cat's
torso will be about four times the length of the
head, and the tail will be about two times the
head length.

Notice that the hind legs are much longer than
the forelegs, and that both pairs of legs are
shorter than the body length.

Kittens

Cats and kittens have somewhat different
proportions. A kitten's head is much larger in
relation to its body than a full-grown cat's. Its
neck is shorter, and its ears may seem larger in
proportion to the rest of its body. Its legs are
short and wide, and its feet may seem bigger
compared to its body.

A kitten's face has different proportions, as well.
Its eyes are big, and its mouth and nose are
smaller.

When seen standing in
profile, a kitten's body is
about two times the
length of its head (*left*). In
an adult cat in this pose, it
is about four times the
head length (*below*)

These two drawings
were done in B pencil
on tracing paper

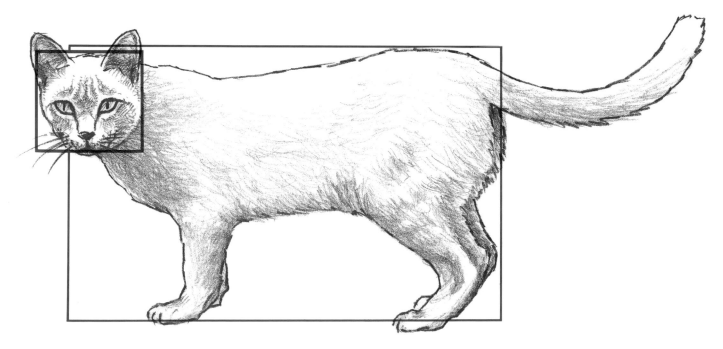

Light and Shade

To convey the sense of a cat's shape, explore the way light bounces and reflects off its surface. This appears on the cat's surface as a range of tones, from white through greys to very black, that create highlights and shadows showing receding and protruding surfaces.

Observe carefully, and understand the source and strength of the light. Strong, direct light creates dark shadows. Light from several directions will produce softer, less dark areas of shadow.

The light shining on the sphere (*above left*) comes from the top left, making the left side bright and the right side darker, as it is in shadow. Similarly with the cat beside it. Light falling from the top left picks out areas of brightness – these are areas that are closest to the source of light. Areas further away, or those where the light doesn't reach, are darker

Like the sphere above, the cat's head (*left*) receives strong light from the top left. Notice that the right eye, which is away from the light, is darker than the left eye. To make your drawing natural, you must carry through the light and shade logic to all elements

Using tone in shapes

Start with just a few tones – such as white and a few shades of grey. As you practise and become more confident, you will learn how to use a wider range of tones to give a sense of colour.

Shadow studies are best done using the block method. Draw your first sketch as though the cat were made of cardboard, with different planes at various angles to the light.

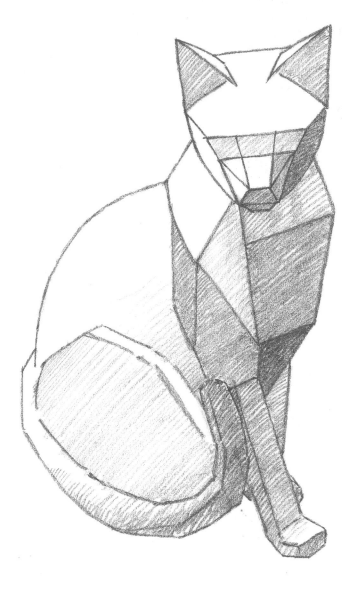

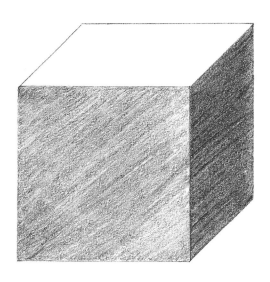

Use a narrow range of tones to shade in the planes that are away from the light, with even darker tones for areas, like the belly, which are also cast in shadow by nearby body parts.

The blocky cat (*above* and *left*) makes it easier to see how areas of the cat's surface are affected by the light or lack of it. Like the cube, which receives strong, direct light from the top left, the top and left side of the cat's body and head are brightest, and the right side and bottom are darkest

Structure and Form

When you draw the full figure of a cat it helps if you think of a number of different aspects of the creature while you work. On these pages you'll find several ways of visualizing a cat's shape.

The silhouette cat
You can probably clearly see the outline shape of the cat, but looking at a silhouette, in which the shape is filled in solid, helps you see proportions more clearly

The skeleton cat
You don't need to study general anatomy, but knowing a little about how the legs are jointed or the feet touch the ground helps you understand the basic frame of the figure

The matchstick cat
Although a very simple way of visualizing a cat's structure, the matchstick figure helps you see clearly the position of the feet and the general posture of the cat

The tin-can cat
Using tubes and other simple geometric shapes can be helpful when trying to create a three-dimensional appearance and when drawing views that are foreshortened or unusual

The main picture of a striped tabby was drawn using HB pencil and finger smudging on thick cartridge paper. It was essential first to get the basic shape right, as the cat's underlying form affects the way the stripes appear in its fur

1

You might feel overwhelmed by the complexity of the cat's form, especially when trying to draw it from a difficult angle. But a cat, like any other living creature or inanimate object, can be thought of as the sum of its individual parts. Think of each part as a familiar shape – a circle, a square, an oval, a triangle. This will make it easier to tackle even the most complex pose.

Practising using shapes

Approach the drawing in stages. Begin with a rough sketch that conveys the basic form and pose in simple shapes (**1**). At each stage add more detail, starting with the eyes and face (**2, 3**) and then completing the details of the body (**4**).

Seeing shapes in poses

The half-sitting, half-standing pose is a common one for cats. For the two sketches opposite, I used overlapping circles for the head and body to get the basic shape, and triangles for ears.

It's usually easier to practise cats' shapes by drawing short-haired cats. Once you feel more confident, try drawing a long-haired cat, like a Persian, using simple shapes. It's harder to see the form beneath all the fur!

2

3

4

Notice all the familiar geometric shapes in the walking cat (*left*). Drawing it in boxy shapes helped me to focus on the difficulty of capturing perspective without getting caught up in the details

The cats on these pages were all drawn in HB and B pencils on cartridge paper

Heads and Facial Features

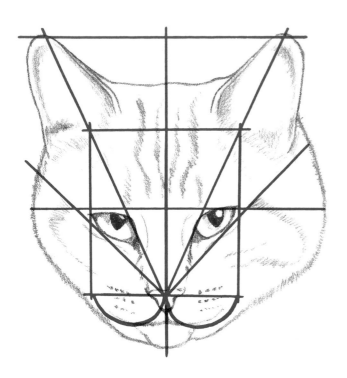

All cats share the basic facial features – eyes, ears, nose, mouth, whiskers – and the same basic relationship among these features. Viewed from the front, this relationship can be shown by breaking down the face into a simple pattern of lines (*left*). Start with a central vertical line which divides the face in half. Then add horizontal lines at regular intervals: top of ears, forehead, above the eyes, at the nose. This is a kind of ladder, with each rung the same distance from the next. Add two more vertical lines at the outside edge of the eyes, then add diagonal lines that intersect this central grid and radiate toward the edge of the face. These relationships are constant. Although there will be some variation among individual cats, use this as the basic model for all frontal cat faces.

Cats of different species have different-shaped heads. Siamese and Burmese cats, for example, have wedge-shaped heads, narrow at the bottom and wider at the top (*right*). Manx and Persians are examples of cats with round heads (*far right*). For both types, begin with a basic circle for the face, and refine the shape as you work

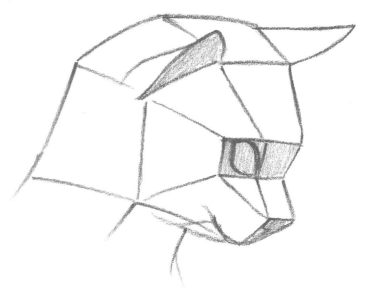

In these blocked heads, the planes of the eyes, the front of the ears, and the end of the nose are parallel. They have been darkened here to emphasize this feature. No matter which way the cat turns its head, these planes will remain parallel.

The nose, however, is closer to you than the eyes. You must show it as foreshortened, so that it appears to protrude beyond the other planes to which it is parallel

Perspective

Although the arrangement of facial features is constant, it appears to change when the face is viewed at an angle. When a cat is seen in three-quarter view, for example, its features are seen in perspective, making the eye further away seem smaller than the one closer to you. When viewing a cat in profile, you won't be able to see all of its facial features. But you must always imagine the side you cannot see.

Use the blocking method to practise head forms. Think of the head in terms of planes at angles to one another. Planes that are parallel will remain parallel at any angle. Planes that are closer to you will appear foreshortened.

Draw helping lines in faint pencil wherever you need them as guides to placement – they can always be erased later. And continually check the relationship among the facial features as you work.

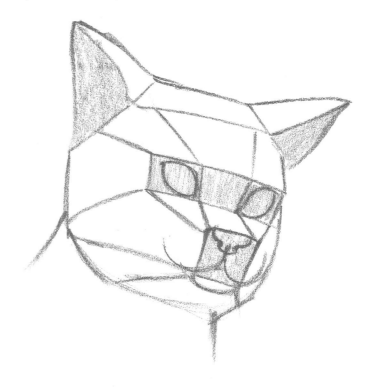

Before you draw your cat's face, it is helpful to learn some basic guidelines.

• Use geometric shapes. Seen from the front, a cat's face is either circular or wedge shaped. Its eyes are also circular, but its nose is triangular.

• Use symmetry. A cat's face, like our own, is symmetrical. It is essential to remember this symmetry when you plot the positions of the eyes, ears and cheeks in a drawing that is not a direct frontal view.

1–2 Begin with a simple freehand circle, divided into quarters with lines down and across the centre. Use the cross lines as the frame on which to locate the eyes, nose and mouth

3–4 Remember that the eyes appear about halfway up the face. Draw them

first as circles on the line across the centre, then add diagonal lines to show where the brow begins

5 The nose is triangular and is about midway between the horizontal cross line and the chin

6 Place the mouth about midway between the nose and the chin

Construction
Here is a step-by-step sequence to help you plot the positions of the features on an imaginary cat's face. Do your construction in a soft pencil (3B or 2B) so that

these lines are faint and can either be erased carefully or hidden under the detail you add later

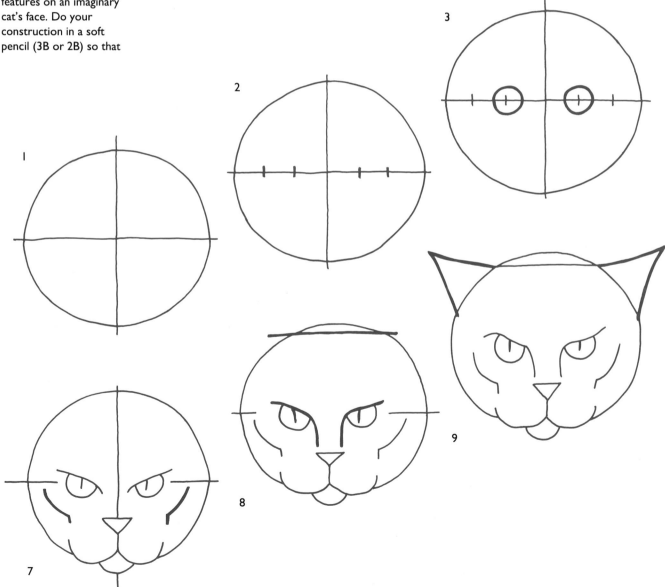

7–10 Now add other lines to define the face, including cheeks and ears. The cheeks add shape, giving the cat's face a ball-like appearance

11–12 Final touches include filling in the pupils and adding whiskers, and going over your final outline with ragged lines to give the appearance of fur. Cats' whiskers grow in regular rows

Cats' eyes
A cat's pupils change their shape dramatically with the amount of light falling on the cat's face (*right*). Unlike our pupils (which change size but not shape), a cat's pupils turn into vertical oval slits when it is looking into a bright light

Side view
A cat's face looks flat from the front but its gentle contours can be seen from a side view (*far right*). The eyes are not sunk deep into the face, but the forehead is rounded and the nose protrudes slightly from the front of the cat's face

Surface Texture

Building surface texture

Texture is one of the most important aspects of drawing cats. It is also one of the most enjoyable tasks, as the great variety of fur textures – long-haired, short-haired, wire-haired – offers room for experimentation and exploration.

Carefully observe the surface of the cat you are drawing. Can you tell what its fur feels like simply by looking? Notice also that a cat has several different textures: its collar might be woolly, its paws less hairy, its cheeks and forehead soft and downy, its eyes shiny and smooth. You can portray these different types of textures using various techniques. Smudge with your finger to create a soft, blended effect. Use the smoothness or roughness of the paper to enhance the texture, as with the Siamese opposite whose coat is smooth and softened using finger smudging, bringing out the underlying texture of the paper.

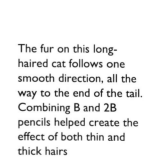

The fur on this long-haired cat follows one smooth direction, all the way to the end of the tail. Combining B and 2B pencils helped create the effect of both thin and thick hairs

The long-haired cat (*left*) is woolly even around the face. This was drawn in 2B pencil on Bockingford paper

The sleekness of the Siamese's fur was captured using conté crayon on Ingres paper (*below*)

When drawing long-haired texture, be sure to make your strokes in the direction of the fur. This is not always the same direction: the fur on the face of the cat above goes in many different directions.

Invented texture
Texture doesn't have to match exactly that of the subject. You can invent textures to create interesting, unusual effects. One way to do this is to place your paper over a textured surface – sandpaper or wood, for example – and gently rub with a pencil, as if doing a brass rubbing. Coarse textures can add a liveliness to your drawing. Be careful, though, not to rub too hard or you might damage your paper.
Experiment with ways of producing different invented textures.

Fur Markings

Coats and fur

Fur types and markings do much to distinguish one type of cat from another. Some of the differences are quite dramatic – a shaggy, long-haired Persian contrasts well with a sleek, short-haired Siamese. Or a cat's fur may be a combination of short and long hair.

In addition to hair length, other aspects of cats' coats are colour and markings. Colours range from lilac, blue and grey to cream, orange, chocolate and black, with many shades in between.

A prize, long-haired red Persian is large and relatively free of striped markings. I drew this in HB, 2B and 4B pencils on tracing paper

The regular stripes of the American short-haired tabby cover the full extent of its body, from face to tail. Only the paws remain stripeless. It was drawn in 2B pencil on Ingres paper

A Siamese is usually light brown or grey with darker areas around the face, legs and tail ('seal points'). Its short hair makes for smooth, sleek lines. This one (*below*) was drawn in dip pen and ink on watercolour paper

Fur markings can be fun to draw, since there are many different types: clean or blotchy stripes, spots or patches, even tortoiseshell, a sort of patchwork of black and orange. Observe the markings carefully – often they don't cover the cat's entire body.

You can experiment with fur and markings by drawing a simple cat outline and photocopying it several times. Use these outlines to practise drawing long and short hair and various markings.

Portraying Expressions

Catching cats' expressions is hardest of all. Every cat not only has distinctive features but distinctive expressions as well. Compare the two large pictures on these pages. The cat on the left has a watchful, almost wary stare. The cat on the right, though in a similar pose, has a more curious look, as if eager to play.

One way to practise this task is to make quick sketches of different expressions as you see them. Try to capture the emotion by examining how it changes the features of a cat's face.

The eyes give clues that are useful when drawing cats' faces. You can tell this cat (*below*) is looking into a bright light because its pupils appear as narrow slits. Its expression is a watchful one

The cats on these pages were drawn using 2B and 4B pencils on different papers.
Notice the difference in expressions, especially between the somewhat wary cat (*below*) and the hissing cat (*bottom*)

Cats communicate through facial expression; by observation, you will learn how emotions change the appearance of cats' facial features. A happy cat, for instance, perks its ears up; a frightened cat lays its ears flat. Sometimes this will be obvious: a fierce, angry cat, for example, will narrow its eyes and widen its mouth.

Even quick sketches convey much about a cat. Pay attention to the shape of the eyes, ears and mouth – as in these four sketches. These were drawn in B pencil on Kent paper

Sometimes the changes are more subtle. The slight lowering of a cat's head, for example, could indicate that it is unsure if a newcomer is a friend or foe, or, when combined with narrowed eyes, could signal pleasure at being petted.

Cats and kittens show different expressions. A kitten's expression may be one of dumbfounded curiosity, compared to the often wise and composed expressions of older cats. This maturity is also often seen in large, wild cats.

Many adult domestic cats show the same solemn expression as some wild cats, like the jaguar (*above*). Notice the differences and similarities in facial features, especially in the shape of the eyes

The drawing of the wide-eyed Persian (*left*) was done in 2B pencil on tracing paper

35

Sketching

The cat's fur is the most prominent aspect of this drawing, done on watercolour paper in mixed media — 4B pencil, water-soluble pencil and brush, and dip pen and ink

Improving your drawing

Cats are a challenging subject – unless they're
sleeping, they usually don't keep still for long.
It's likely you won't have a chance to complete a
detailed drawing at one time. You'll need
patience and lots of practice.

Keeping a **sketchbook** is the best way to practise
drawing cats. Don't worry if you have pages of
drawings you have had to abandon midway;
you can always return to them. Try drawing a
cat from different angles to understand how its
body works.

At this point it's important not to get caught up
in capturing the detail; this can be added later.
Try concentrating on just one aspect of the cat:
its form, fur, expression, or a gesture.

The Siamese cat stayed in
this pose for an unusually
long ten minutes, allowing
me to produce a quite
detailed study of its
form using subtle
shading obtained with
watercolour

I abandoned and returned
to this sketch (*top*)
several times as the cat
moved, but eventually I
captured its pose and the
half-turn of its head. I
used dip pen and ink
washes on thick
cartridge paper

I used quick strokes in B
pencil on cartridge paper
to capture the light and
shade in this cat's
reclining position (*left*)

Be prepared to make many quick sketches to capture the form and energy of the cat. Keep your sketchbook with you and use it to compile a bank of different cat images. One drawing might be a composite of several sketches made at different times.

You can also build up a sketch in different stages. Start with the most basic form, drawing as much of it as you can before the cat changes its pose. You can add to this from memory, defining the cat's pose and then adding details such as facial features.

You can also create a drawing of a group of cats using different sketches from your sketchbook. Overlap them in a way that seems natural so that it appears you drew them all at once.

In this sequence (*above* and *right*), I first drew a quick, rough outline of the cat in my sketchbook while it was in this pose. Using soft pencil on thick cartridge paper, I added detail from memory. I then completed the drawing using dip pen and ink, smudging some areas with my fingertip

These drawings from my sketchbook show the different ways you can use individual sketches

The two poses of the same cat (*top*) were drawn in soft pencil. They were both only half finished before the cat moved on, but I can use them for reference purposes or complete the detail at a later stage

The group of Siamese cats (*right*) is actually the same cat. I used pencil sketches of the cat in three different poses and arranged them to form a new, natural composition, drawn in charcoal

Framing and Composition

Composition is the arrangement and placement of different elements on your drawing surface. You decide how to compose your illustration; it doesn't have to match what you see or how you see it.

Within a single photograph or illustration are several possibilities for compositions. When deciding on your subject, think of the impact you want to make. You can draw cats alone or in a group. You can also choose to draw only part of a cat, such as the head, for a particular emphasis.

Framing
To help you decide, use the framing method. Make two L-shapes from a piece of card and hold them at right angles over different parts of your subject or picture. Move this frame around, and change its shape to a larger square or even a rectangle.

You can also use your hands to frame your composition. Hold them, palms flat out, with the thumbs extended and touching, and place them over different areas of the subject or picture.

Consider the balance of the different elements. When drawing a group, you might want to rearrange each cat to improve on the shape of the overall composition. Consider the focus of the drawing as well.

I wanted to focus on an unusual cat expression so I drew only the face of the hissing tabby.

Narrowing the focus in this case gave the drawing added power. I used HB pencil on cartridge paper

Using grids
You might want to do rough sketches first to plan the best positioning. Once you have a rough sketch, draw a grid of faint pencil lines over it and over your drawing surface. You can then use this grid to transfer the individual elements to your final drawing, allowing you to maintain the balance and proportion as planned.

This series of sketches of a cat washing itself was done in fineline felt-tip pen on layout paper. I experimented with different angles before deciding on the best one for my final composition

The Siamese cat and her three kittens (*above*) make an interesting composition together. They can also be split up into several different compositions. Consider, for example, focusing on the face of one kitten as a separate composition on its own. This was drawn in B pencil on cartridge paper

Domestic Cats

Most domestic cats today are either longhairs or shorthairs. Within these two groups, however, are many different breeds, and within each breed are several varieties.

Although all share the same basic body features and some characteristics – such as curiosity and independence – they also display a great range of differences in appearance and behaviour.

The areas of colour on a Siamese get darker as the cat ages, and its elegance is enhanced. This somewhat stylized drawing of a Siamese (*below*) was done in fineline felt-tip marker on layout paper

Persians, for example, are heavy-set and are gentle, adaptable cats. North American shorthairs are hardy and calm. Abyssinians have an unusual, lively look and lithe frames.

This striped tabby kitten was hard to capture on paper – most kittens are excitable and their movements are skittish. For this drawing (*right*) I used H pencil on tracing paper

The easily distinguished Manx cat (*above*) is not only tailless, but its hind section is higher than its front. This gives the Manx its great leaping ability and its peculiar appearance, enhanced in this drawing by the cat's arched back. This was drawn using 2B pencil on watercolour paper

Observe as many types and breeds of cats as possible. You'll soon begin to spot differences among them that will make your drawings more natural and true to life.

Wild Cats

Wild cats cover an even wider range than domestic cats. They are usually divided into large cats – such as the lion, leopard, tiger and jaguar – and small cats, with the cheetah in its own group. Some, like the lion, have strong, heavy frames. Others are quite small – the ocelot, for example, is only about twice the size of the typical domestic cat. (The cats on these pages, all on cartridge paper in different media, are not drawn to scale.)

A Pallas's cat (*above*) in B pencil

A caracal, with distinctive tufted ears, in coloured pencil (*right*)

The slender African serval in 2B pencil

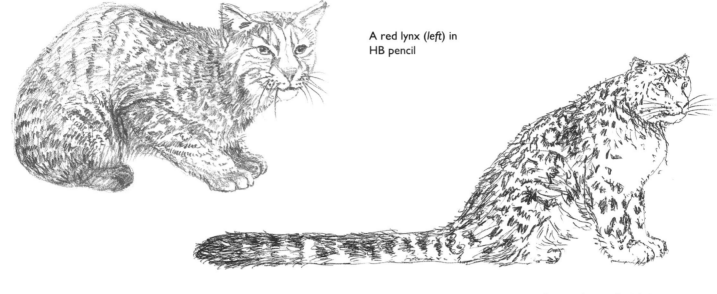

A red lynx (*left*) in
HB pencil

A snow leopard with its
heavy tail (*above*) in ball-
point pen

The fastest animal, a
cheetah (*left*), in fineline
felt-tip marker

A tiger, one of the largest
cats, in coloured
pencil (*below*)

Like domestic cats, wild cats display a variety of
interesting patterns: spots, patches, stripes and
even, as on the jaguar, large rosettes. Often the
pattern doesn't cover the entire animal. Also, no
two animals have identical markings.

Look through nature magazines to find pictures
of wild animals, or – for a bigger challenge – go
to the zoo and draw them from life!

45

Cat Behaviour

Cats sleeping

Cats sleep for up to two-thirds of their lives, so at some point you're likely to want to draw a sleeping cat. This is the ideal occasion for practising the cat's form, as it is sure to be still for at least a short time. Take advantage of the moment!

You won't always have time for detailed drawings, however. Cats usually take several brief 'catnaps' during the day, so it is still important to do quick sketches to try to capture the pose before the cat moves.

The two cosy tabbies (*above*) were drawn in ball-point pen on cartridge paper

These mounds of fur are really a sleeping tortoiseshell cat (*above*) and a tabby kitten and its solid-coloured mother (*left*), all drawn on cartridge paper in HB pencil

A red tabby shorthair caught at the moment just before falling into a deep sleep, drawn in B pencil (*above*), and fast asleep, drawn in ball-point pen (*below*)

One difficulty with drawing sleeping cats is that they are often tightly curled up so they resemble shapeless furry bundles. Remember what you know about the cat's underlying form – its basic anatomy – even if you cannot see it clearly in your subject.

The pattern on this silver tabby (*right*) becomes even more interesting when the cat is wrapped tightly into a ball. It was drawn on cartridge paper in 4B pencil

Stationary cats

It may be difficult to move from drawing still, sleeping cats to capturing active cats in motion. The two tasks are very different. One way to ease this transition is to experiment with stationary cat activities, such as washing and eating. These activities are slower than action and so are less demanding, but the slight motion that is involved adds a sense of movement to the lines of your drawing.

Grooming

Each cat has its own grooming routine. Most, however, wash themselves by licking their paws and rubbing them over their face and ears. If you watch carefully over a period of time, you'll learn to predict the cat's next grooming move. This will also help if you need to refine your drawing later from memory.

Eating

Eating involves little movement, and it is a pose cats stay in for several minutes, making it useful for practice.

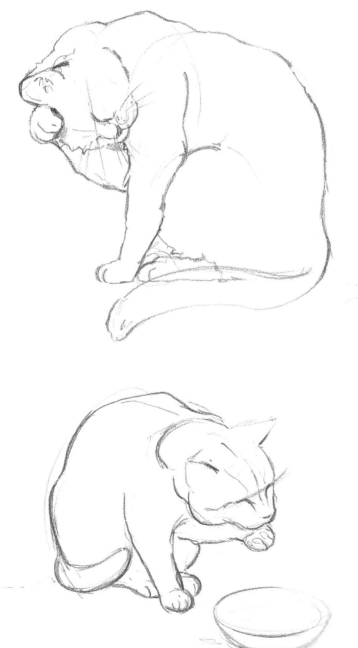

A cat's paws and head are the most important body parts in the grooming ritual. You can almost feel the movement in these sketches: washing the forehead (*top left*), in B pencil on cartridge paper; licking the paw clean (*left*), in B pencil on cartridge paper; and grooming the whiskers and face fur (*above*), in 2B pencil on cartridge paper

Most cats use the same general pose when drinking from a saucer. Tempt your subject cat to adopt this pose by putting down a saucer of milk. Then observe the pose from several different angles, noting the position of the paws and even of the tail. The face, also, is quite different from this angle.

Use careful observation and make quick, frequent sketches to get the basic form. Remember, you can always fill in details later.

I made several quick sketches of this bi-colour shorthair as it drank from its saucer. Sketching from several angles — here from behind (*above*) and from in front (*below*), both in B pencil on cartridge paper — helped me to understand the basic shape of the pose

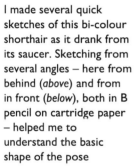

A slightly more detailed sketch of the same cat drinking (*above*) resulted from several unfinished efforts. This one was drawn in 2B pencil on cartridge paper

Cats in action

Watching cats move is a pleasure. Their grace, even in sudden moves, can be difficult to capture on paper, however. It helps to understand something about how a cat moves. Observe the way it walks: which feet move and in what order. Knowing the basics of cat movement will make your action drawings more real and believable.

Catwalk basics

Cats move in a great variety of ways: they prowl, leap, run and walk. Here are a few basics to keep in mind.

● When walking, a cat moves in the following sequence: right rear leg, right front leg, left rear leg, left front leg, and so on.

The sequence here (*above* and *right*) shows a nearly grown kitten first playing with its prey, then pouncing. Drawing a sequence gives a sense of fluidity. I drew this in 2B pencil on cartridge paper

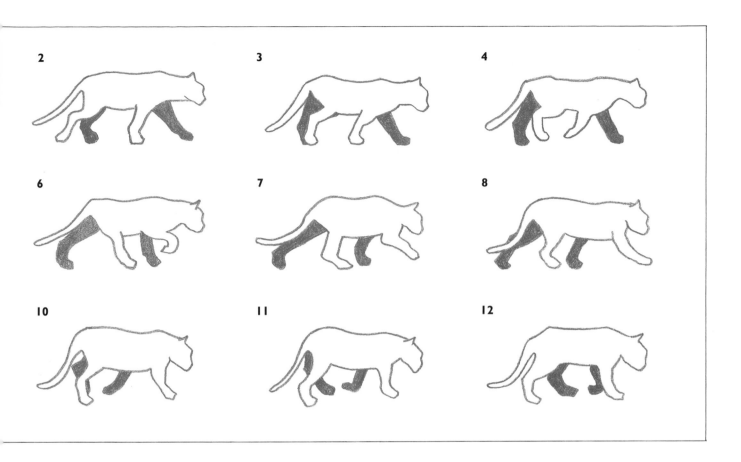

The twelve steps of a cat's walk (*above*). I shaded in the legs on the opposite side of the cat to make it more clear which legs move when

- A walking or running cat will always have two feet on the ground, and even when pouncing, cats often keep their rear paws firmly on the ground.
- A cat's tracks appear almost as a straight line because a cat carefully places one foot in front of the other.

Sequencing

One way to capture action is to draw a sequence. Each new stage of your sequence will show a slightly different pose as the cat moves. To do this, make rapid sketches, one after the other, moving from one unfinished sketch to another. You won't have time to finish a drawing, complete with detail, for each stage. Instead, focus on capturing the form and essence of the movement. Add details of texture and shading later.

Cats in Settings

Drawing cats in their environment is a good way to convey more information to your viewers. You can describe a cat's habits, likes and dislikes, or simply its unusual behaviour by placing the cat in context. Some cats, for example, are only indoor cats. Others roam at will outdoors, either in the garden or around the neighbourhood.

Cats are very independent creatures. During the day, they spend a lot of time alone, perhaps sunning themselves on a nearby roof or watching the world from a window. At night, outdoor cats tend to go around in groups. Even then, however, cats maintain their strong sense of personal space – each cat has its own special territory.

This Turkish Angora balancing on a wooden fence (*left*) was drawn in HB, B and 2B pencils on watercolour paper

If you observe cats in their settings you'll notice characteristics peculiar to cats. They have flexible skeletons and so can squeeze into and around awkward spaces. Also, their tails act as balancing poles, allowing them to walk on quite narrow walls at a great height.

You might want to draw a basket or other bedding material to give your sketch of a sleeping cat added interest (see the following pages for an example). Other domestic items that help create a setting for your indoor cat drawing are scratching posts, sunny windowsills and other spots where cats position themselves.

These Rex cats gathered on the cellar stairs seem to have been caught unawares. I drew them on Bockingford paper using B, 2B and 4B pencils

When drawing a cat in its environment,
construct the setting in the same way as you
would construct the cat. Among the tips you
have learned are drawing verticals and
horizontals, using pencil measuring to test your
accuracy, and finding familiar geometric shapes
in the subject's form. Start with a simple outline
and build on it, working on cat and setting
together so that you maintain the correct
proportion between the two.

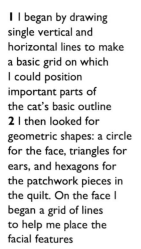

1 I began by drawing
single vertical and
horizontal lines to make
a basic grid on which
I could position
important parts of
the cat's basic outline
2 I then looked for
geometric shapes: a circle
for the face, triangles
for ears, and hexagons for
the patchwork pieces in
the quilt. On the face I
began a grid of lines
to help me place the
facial features

3 Time now for some
details. I added the facial
features and the
beginnings of fur

4

The straight lines of this young exotic shorthair's fur (*above*) contrast nicely with the mix of floral patterns in the patchwork quilt. It isn't always necessary to complete the detail down to the last leaf or hair; sometimes merely suggesting a pattern is enough. This way it keeps your drawing from becoming too cluttered.

4 Once I felt sure of my outline, and before continuing, I erased any unwanted lines. Then I finished off the cat's fur, adding light and shade, and drew in patterns on the quilt

Working from Photographs

Enhancing what you see is an essential part of drawing from photographs. For this cat (*below*), drawn in 2B pencil on watercolour paper, I removed any background in order to emphasize the contrast in light and dark and the furriness of the edges. I paid careful attention to drawing its fur, which is obscured in the original photograph (*left*)

Using photographs as references allows you access to a wide range of subject material, since not everything you might want to draw is available for posing. You might, for instance, want to draw a group of kittens, but you know of only one adult cat you can draw from life. You can also draw invented compositions: groups of cats or cats in imagined settings, or even a mix of cats from different photographs.

Use photographs you find in magazines, books, and even your family album if you have a cat.

Drawing from photographs doesn't mean simply copying. You can, and should, improve on what you see in photographs by emphasizing certain aspects – such as fur markings or expressions – in your final drawing. Remember that you are drawing solid, rounded objects, not flat surfaces, and try to inject into your drawing a liveliness that might not be evident in the original photograph.

Don't be embarrassed to draw from photographs. It is a good way to practise difficult tasks and to build your confidence for capturing expressions from life studies.

Looking After Your Drawings

Fixing

Protect your final drawing by spraying it with a fixative. This is especially important with drawings done in pencil, pastel, crayon or charcoal, which smudge easily.

To fix your drawing, use a spray can or a mouth-blown diffuser. Spray the fixative evenly across the entire surface from about 30–40cm (12–16in) away. Once it is dry, spray again lightly all over.

Storing

After fixing your drawing, if not displaying it immediately, store it carefully. Lay it flat with a piece of tissue paper on either side to protect it from damage.

This tabby cat was drawn on coloured Ingres paper in pastel

This Persian was
drawn using 6B pencil on
textured Kent paper.
Both drawings on these
pages needed to be
sprayed with a fixative
before being stored or
displayed

Using Your Drawings

Cats are wonderful images to use on birthday cards. You can achieve surprising humour by combining, for example, a serious drawing of a cat with funny words

Cards

You can give much pleasure to friends and family by personalizing cards and other items with your cat drawings. On these pages are described a few ways of using your artwork, but there are many more. The possibilities are almost limitless.

Keep in mind that your drawing style is unique. You don't always have to use realism to try to convey a photo-perfect image of your subject. Other styles – such as comic strips or bold outlines – are also suitable for using on cards, posters, notepaper and other printed materials.

You can also make unique holiday cards using your cat drawings, like this Christmas card

COME TO OUR PARTY

Saturday 16th February, at 7.00PM at 24 Manor Road, Oxford

Invitations to parties and other special events are also made more exciting with your artwork. Be sure to include all the details, including time, date and place, in a clear and straightforward way

YOU ARE INVITED ATTEND PETER'S PARTY

8.30pm FRIDAY 9 JUNE

THE BEACH HOUSE PALM BOULEVARD

R·S·V·P

Bookmarks are simple to produce and they make excellent gifts. Simply cut out a rectangular piece of cardboard on which to do your cat drawing. To preserve it, laminate it with plastic

When producing artwork for printing, try to use simple and clean images. Colour is more expensive to print than black and white. Strong bold lines and areas of stark black and white tend to reproduce better than tones, but finely detailed pieces can also work. Experiment first by photocopying your drawing to see how well it copies. You'll soon learn what adjustments you need to make to get the best results.

Other ways to use your artwork include personalized stationery, advertising posters and notices, and newspaper articles.

Stationery

Design a personalized letterhead by printing or photocopying one of your cat drawings on standard stationery paper. You could use it for business or personal correspondence as a way to convey something about you to the recipient.

Here are two types of stationery decorated with cats. Simple outlines can be used to create a lively decorative border

Boldi Strasse 70
CH - 4381 Nussbaumen
6. Baden

3 Perrins Court Highgate High St London N6

No one would pass this poster without giving it a second look! The use of a powerful image helps when you want to get the viewer's attention

A newspaper article is livened up by the addition of original cat drawings (*below*)

CAT PEOPLE

THE ORIGINAL 1951 FILM
A SPECIAL SHOWING FOR TWO NIGHTS ONLY
THE UNIVERSITY THEATRE 22 & 23 MARCH: 7.30pm

SEATS NOT BOOKABLE

Posters and newspapers
Use a bold image to decorate a large poster. These are real attention-grabbers and are a good way to get your artwork noticed. Smaller, less bold images work well combined with a lot of text, as in a newspaper or magazine article.